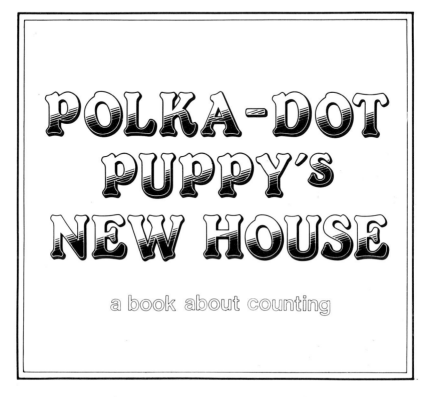

POLKA-DOT PUPPY'S NEW HOUSE

a book about counting

by Janet McDonnell
illustrated by Linda Hohag
and Lori Jacobson

Created by

THE CHILD'S WORLD

Distributed by CHILDRENS PRESS®
Chicago, Illinois

CHILDRENS PRESS HARDCOVER EDITION
ISBN 0-516-05609-3
CHILDRENS PRESS PAPERBACK EDITION
ISBN 0-516-45609-1

Library of Congress Cataloging in Publication Data

McDonnell, Janet, 1962-
  Polka-Dot Puppy's new house : a book about counting / by Janet
McDonnell ; illustrated by Linda Hohag.
     p. cm.
  Summary: Despite the advice of a multitude of other animals on
how many windows to include in his new house, Polka-Dot Puppy
decides on his own. Illustrations of each group of animals and the
windows in their houses provide practice in counting.
  ISBN 0-89565-380-X
  [1. Dogs—Fiction.   2. Animals—Fiction.   3. Dwellings—Fiction.
4. Counting.]   I. Hohag, Linda, ill.   II. Title.
PZ7.M478436Po   1988
[E]—dc19   88-11941
                                                               CIP
                                                                AC

1 2 3 4 5 6 7 8 9 10 11 12 R 96 95 94 93 92 91 90 89 88

POLKA-DOT PUPPY'S NEW HOUSE

a book about counting

Polka-Dot Puppy was planning
to build a new house. "Hmmm,"
he wondered. "How many
windows will I need?"

"I know," said one wise owl from
a tree nearby. "I know just how
many windows you should have."

"How many?" asked Polka-Dot
Puppy.

5

"I have one wonderful window,"
said the owl. "It is just enough.
I can look out and the sun can
look in. One is all you need."

"One window!" cried two turtles, passing by. "No, no, no. You should have two.

"Look at our house. You can see
why you'll need two. You'll need
one to look out in the morning
and one to look out at night."

"Only two windows in a house?"
chirped three thrushes. "But you
will need at least three.

"In our house, we need three windows so we can watch the clouds pass by. We need all three to see them."

"But, Polka-Dot Puppy, you will
need more," said four foxes.

"How will you keep your new
house cool unless you have four
windows, as we do? They let the
cool breeze in all day. Yes, you
need four windows."

"You'll need more than four,"
croaked five frogs.

"In Lily Pad Place, we have five
windows. They let in flies for us
to catch. Trust us. You need five."

"Sssssilly frogs," said six snakes
in the grass.

"Polka-Dot Puppy can't have
just five windows. He will need
sssssix. Sssssix windows let in
lots of ssssunshine."

"Don't listen to those snakes,"
said seven squirrels. "You will
be much happier with seven
windows.

"With seven windows, you can
bake seven pies and put them
on the windowsills to cool."

"Seven windows will never do,"
said eight ermines. "Eight would
be just right for you.

"We have eight windows in our home, four on top and four on bottom."

"But why have eight when you could have nine?" asked nine newts.

"Our nine windows are so much fun. We climb in and out of them all day long."

"Nine windows? That would be
all wrong!" ten turkeys gobbled.
"All the best houses have ten
windows.

"Our house has ten windows—
all quite tiny. And we always
keep them clean and shiny."

"Ten tiny, shiny windows?" asked
Polka-Dot Puppy. "My, oh my,
that is a lot.

"Now what should I do?" Polka-Dot Puppy wondered. "Everyone tells me something different. They all think their number is the best."

As Polka-Dot Puppy sat there
wondering, one wise owl, two
turtles, and . . .

his other animal friends began
to gather around him.

"Welllll, . . ." they all said. "What
number will it be?"

Polka-Dot Puppy looked at the
one wise owl, two turtles, three
thrushes, four foxes, five frogs,
six snakes, seven squirrels,

eight ermines, nine newts, and
ten turkeys. "I have picked the
number," he said.

"How many?" asked his friends.

"ZERO!" said Polka-Dot Puppy.
"All a Polka-Dot Puppy really
needs is a door and nothing
more!"